Old LARKHALL

by
James Hamilton

The 'caller' gives a demonstration of his technique for advertising what was on at the Empire Theatre. He is standing alongside an advertisement board on wheels carrying posters for a film called *The Scarlet Car* starring Franklyn Farnum.

© James Hamilton 2001
First published in the United Kingdom, 2001,
reprinted 2005, 2011, 2012
by Stenlake Publishing Ltd.
01290 551122
www.stenlake.co.uk

ISBN 9781840331745

ACKNOWLEDGEMENTS

Very many thanks for assistance with historical research to Alan Newlands, and for information and use of photographs to Agnes Baillie, Ambrose Burns, Kathleen Brannigan, David Cross, Mary Davidson, Maggie Deans, Boyd Falconer, George Feeney, Tom Miller, Hugh Walker, Russell Wallace, Gavin Wilson and Jenny Wilson.

The publishers would like to thank Robert Grieves for providing the pictures on pages 46 and 47.

FURTHER READING

The books listed below were used by the author during his research. None of them are available from Stenlake Publishing. Those interested in finding out more are advised to contact their local bookshop or reference library.

Statistical Account of Scotland, 1791 (available on the internet at http://edina.ac.uk/StatAcc/)
New Statistical Account of Scotland, 1845 (available on the internet at http://edina.ac.uk/StatAcc)
Third Statistical Account of Scotland, 1960
Larkhall; Its Historical Development (project by Larkhall Academy), 1979
Larkhall Victualling Society, 1821–1921
Various publications of Larkhall Heritage Group
Down the Mine at Twelve; A Netherburn Boyhood, George Anderson
Bygone Larkhall, Richard Stenlake (out of print)

VIDEOS

History of Dalserf Parish, Rosebank Productions
Larkhall: Then and Now, James Hamilton

Many localities can boast of residents who were famous warriors, adventurers or members of the nobility; Larkhall's best-known son is Robert Smillie, venerated for his lifelong toil for his fellow workers. Born in Ireland in 1857, he came to settle in Scotland, starting work at the age of nine years as a message boy and entering the pits where his first job was supervising a water pump. After a period as a coal hewer, his fellow workers voted him to be the checkweighman to protect their interests. He was elected to serve on Larkhall School Board where he is credited with initiating evening classes. Early in his working life he was heavily involved in trade union activities for the Lanarkshire coal miners, eventually becoming president of the Miners' Federation of Great Britain. He stood as a socialist candidate for parliament on several occasions, and was elected MP for Morpeth from 1923 to 1929. His home remained in Larkhall until his death in 1940. Another locally famous person is James Keir Hardie (1856–1915) from nearby Quarter, who was also a miner. He is credited as being the father of the Labour Party.

INTRODUCTION

Today Larkhall, in the parish of Dalserf, is a thriving village in the administrative area of South Lanarkshire. The town of Hamilton is four miles away to the north, while a journey of less than twenty miles also northwards takes one to Glasgow city centre. As a rough guide the parish of Dalserf is bounded by the Rivers Clyde, Avon and Cander Water.

Not a great deal is known about Larkhall in the distant past and even details about the parish of Dalserf are sketchy. It would appear that around the twelfth and thirteenth centuries, Dalserf parish grew out of lands belonging to the ancient Church of Cadzow (Cadihou). These came to be known as the lands of Machan (Meeheyn), and were subsequently given to or taken over by the forebears of the Hamilton family. Over time they were distributed to the various descendants of the famous ducal house of Hamilton.

During the following hundreds of years the fortunes of the powerful Hamilton family were to increase, and the name of Hamilton was assumed by those who were related to the family by blood or marriage to reinforce and perpetuate their influence. This can be seen in names such as Hamilton of Raploch (at Raploch Castle) and Hamilton of Broomhill (at Broomhill and Machan Moor) and indeed the Hamilton presence is still retained in many Larkhall street names such as Duke Street, Hamilton Street, Raploch Street, Broomhill Place, Machan Road etc.

In the last eighty years the choice of names for thoroughfares in Larkhall has had a more political flavour, reflecting the presence of the working classes on local councils. While recognition was paid to individuals such as Nevison, Parker and Herbison, who had contributed in some way to improving the community, Labour Party figures were also given prominence. Local councillors like William Spiers and John Ewing have been recognised, as well as national leaders such as Keir Hardie, Robert Smillie and Clem Attlee.

One thing that is definitely known about the parish of Dalserf is that fruit growing was established from early times. Orchards flourished on the banks of the Avon at Millheugh and even more so along the Clyde at Dalserf village. The most important crops were plums, then apples and pears. In 1841 it is recorded that 60 varieties of apples and 24 types of pears were grown. The ground beneath the trees was used to grow potatoes, oats, beans, barley and rye.

Millheugh, once separate from Larkhall but now part of the town, owed its development to fruit growing and fishing (salmon were fished until the River Avon became polluted), as well as benefiting from the passing trade brought by travellers en route from Hamilton and Larkhall to Quarter and Stonehouse. Industry arrived in 1796 when a Mr McGregor erected some buildings as a printworks at Avonbank. In 1806 a Mr Marshall from Hawick brought men and materials to convert the building into an inkle (tape) factory, which lasted a short period. Then in 1825 John Burns set up a distillery there, but the flavour of the whisky apparently could not compete with the Highland blends and it had a short life. Messrs John Young & Sons of Glasgow started bleachfield operations there in 1838 and the business was later taken over by D. C. Miller. This continued in some form until twenty years ago when the manufacture of linen for roller blinds came to an end. The machinery used was originally driven by water diverted to the factory along a lade, the outline of which is still visible today alongside the River Avon. Little trace of either these industrial developments or fruit growing at Millheugh is visible today as the land has been given over for the erection of villas and bungalows.

Larkhall's economic development took off in the early eighteenth century. Until that time it consisted of nothing more than a few fermtouns built in a rough circle round the Old Cross. With the Act of Union of 1707, free trade with England began and Larkhall benefited from its position on the main route of the cattle trail running from the north through Glasgow to Carlisle.

Many other factors contributed to Larkhall's continued growth. These included the introduction and expansion of the coaching trade between Glasgow and Carlisle, the agricultural revolution and the granting of 99 year leases on farms around Larkhall. In addition the success of the weaving industry and the subsequent construction of the Ayr to Edinburgh turnpike road (Telford's Turnpike) via Larkhall, meant that the village began to prosper and expand. Until the early nineteenth century and the advent of coal mining, Larkhall was perceived primarily as a flourishing weaving village.

Along with the successful development of the handloom weaving industry came the formation of friendly societies, and Larkhall, in the forefront of progressive thought and action, has been credited as being the cradle of the building society movement. In keeping with the spirit of David Dale and his son-in-law Robert Owen, who established better conditions for their workers in the factories at New Lanark, Larkhall weavers founded their own co-operative society with the high sounding title of Larkhall Victualling Society. Some claim it to be the second oldest co-operative society selling provisions in the world. The development of this society, which allegedly gave drams instead of monetary dividends in the initial years following its formation in 1821, was quite phenomenal. However, some decades later, men keen to promote the temperance movement formed Larkhall Co-operative Society, operating from Montgomery Street. Both societies were based on making provisions available to members at reasonable prices and both eventually paid dividends on purchases made. It is still possible to find people in Larkhall who can quote their co-op shop number, although the societies ceased functioning over thirty years ago.

Just as the handloom weaving industry was receding and losing out to the burgeoning factories, the next significant element in Larkhall's development came along – this was the expansion of coal mining following the opening of a railway link from Ferniegair through Larkhall East, Dalserf and Netherburn to Coalburn in 1856. For over a hundred years from the 1850s railway lines transported coal from around 45 collieries in the vicinity of Larkhall, which were opened and worked for varying periods. By the time of the nationalisation of the coal industry in 1947 Larkhall's richest seams had been exhausted, and the last coal was taken out around 1960.

Coal mining around Larkhall brought a significant investment in communications and infrastructure, which was reflected in the development of railways, the tram system, and the bus network. Rows of miners' houses were built at Merryton, Buffy, Bog and Summerlee to provide accommodation for men from outwith the district taking up employment locally. The main thoroughfare soon abounded with a variety of shops. One aspect of early twentieth century life that is remembered is the number of miners seen going to and from work in their pit clothes, as there were no pit-head baths in those days. By the 1940s most local pits had shut down and miners travelled daily by bus to the collieries at Coalburn, Douglas Water, Shotts and Cardowan. When the seams at these collieries ran out, many of the redundant miners living in Larkhall who did not elect to move to collieries in Ayrshire, the Lothians or in England found employment in the steelworks at Motherwell, particularly Ravenscraig. In the wake of the decline of the coal industry, central government included Lanarkshire as part of the Scottish Development Area and the industrial estate at Strutherhill was created in an effort to boost local employment. Many of its projects employed mainly female labour, however, which did not help to soak up the jobs lost to men in coal mining.

The closure of the collieries foreshadowed the end of the railways, depriving Larkhall of further local jobs. Larkhall East station closed to passenger traffic in 1951, and Larkhall Central in 1965. Passengers had been lured away by the availability and frequency of buses from the early 1920s when regular services were introduced, although these in turn felt the pressure of the private car. A feature in the streets of Larkhall now is the number of taxis, which seem to be used very regularly by residents, especially the younger element.

It was thought that Larkhall's railway age had gone forever. However, there are now regular reports in the newspapers that as Larkhall is the largest centre of population (15,077 according to the 1991 census) without a train service in Scotland, Strathclyde Passenger Transport is to extend the line from Hamilton to Larkhall with intermediate stops at Chatelherault, Ferniegair and Larkhall North.

Religion has always played a significant role in the life of the villagers of Dalserf parish. Dalserf Church, no doubt built on the site of previous religious buildings, bears the date 1655. As Larkhall developed 'tent preaching' began and various churches began to be constructed. Over the past 350 years, denominations and sects including the Covenanters, McMillanites, Church of Scotland, Free Church of Scotland, Relief, United Presbyterian, Baptist, Roman Catholic, Salvation Army, Jehovah's Witnesses and Plymouth Brethren have been represented locally. In common with many towns and villages, the role of the modern church in Larkhall includes the promotion of recreational clubs and leisure activities of all sorts. One has only to think of the various women's guilds, brigades, youth clubs, badminton sections, drama groups, choirs etc. to get the picture. Multiplying this by the number of churches and religious organisations that exist in Larkhall gives an insight into the number and diversity of recreational activities available.

It is sad to reflect that as Larkhall has expanded some of the community spirit of the last two centuries seems to have dissipated. The weavers chose to work together for the good of all and were behind such worthwhile projects as building, sickness and co-operative societies. For decades the miners, brought together by the danger of their work and through the fight for better wages and conditions, built up a marvellous spirit of friendship and self-support, especially during periods of strikes or lockouts when the likes of soup kitchens were provided. Now activities of togetherness such as the annual gala day and 'Larkie Fair' have fallen into desuetude. Sadly the local pipe band and the silver band have also ceased to exist at a time when more money is being spent than ever on providing children at school with instruments and music lessons.

During the two world wars, Larkhall, like the whole of Britain, paid a severe price in the calamitous killing of its men and women and the resultant devastation of their families. The memorials to the parish dead reveal the names and frightening totals; what cannot be recorded is the amount of anguish and heartbreak behind the statistics. The three parish memorials, Larkhall, Ashgill and Netherburn record the names of 307 dead from the First World War and 104 from the Second World War (there may be some duplication of names as the Larkhall Memorial covers the whole of the parish for the 1914/1918 war).

Over the years Larkhall has had its allotted share of sporting groups with football teams galore from schoolboy level to some sponsored by pubs. The principal clubs in the town have been – and still are – Larkhall Thistle and

Royal Albert. Other groups and activities include golf and racquet clubs, cycling, harriers with David Gracie and swimming with Jean Hill, both of whom brought distinction to the village through being chosen to compete for Britain at international level. There have been choirs, groups of entertainers and dancing classes, with the most famous graduate from the community drama group being Una McLean, who has top billing in theatres in Glasgow and Edinburgh.

One elderly lady, Maggie Deans, who was interviewed for this book, recalled the changes in her living conditions over 80 years. She had moved on from a miners' row without piped water or internal WC and only paraffin lamps for illumination, to the home she owns now with the mod cons that we take for granted such as washing machine, microwave and television. She explained how she appreciated the improvement in her lifestyle that her grandchildren accepted as the norm. When she talked to them about her early life, and recalled the lack of basic comforts, they seemed to think she had been born in the Dark Ages. She related how her early memories of entertainment in Larkhall were of magic lantern slide shows, then silent films in the community hall in the days before the village had two cinemas. Her earliest memory of home entertainment was a cumbersome wireless set that depended on a long outside aerial and required the charging of batteries and accumulators, as well as regularly needing replacement valves.

If the compiler may add one aspect of progress in his lifetime, he was taught to write on a slate at primary school before being trusted with using a pencil and then a pen and inkwell. Later developments included the fountain then ball pen. His first typewriter was manual, then electronic models became available. Finally, the pages of this book were prepared on a personal computer with facilities to e-mail words and photographs to correspondents anywhere in the world.

Back row: Tom Collins, unknown, Bert Lockhart, George Hall, unknown, Frank McCorry, Hugh Lockhart, Jim McLeod, Bert Fleming
Front row: unknown, Bob Wilson (President), unknown

This photograph was taken at a Burns Supper organised by the Larkhall Professional and Businessmen's Club and includes members, friends and guest artistes. The late Bob Wilson (who died on 29 March 1974) was a Lanark County Councillor, then Strathclyde Regional Councillor for Larkhall and Stonehouse, holding important posts such as Convenor of Social Work. His son Gavin (proprietor of Burns the Stationers) was President of the Larkhall Professional and Businessmen's Club exactly 30 years after his father held the post.

The small village of Ferniegair lies astride the A72 a mile south of Hamilton and two miles from Larkhall. Until the M74 motorway was opened in 1968 it was on the main trunk road from Glasgow to Carlisle. This picture shows the old miners' rows and the chimney of Ferniegair Colliery. After the 1939–1945 war the pit ceased production and the rows were demolished. The building incorporating the Commercial Bar still stands and is currently home to The Owls restaurant. A former resident recalled her happy childhood in Ferniegair where she attended primary school. She remembered with gratitude Miss Smith, who was a teacher there for her entire working life and also ran the Brownie pack. A feature each summer (and still being held in 2001) was the gala day for Ferniegair and Allanton children, who paraded to the large park beside Chatelherault Inn. All the children had a 'tinny' (small tin mug) attached by white tape round their necks. At the park each child was given tea or milk and a bag of buns before participating in a programme of sports for all age groups.

Ferniegair Church is now only a mission church for the parish of Cadzow due to the decrease in the size of the congregation. Ferniegair was originally a hamlet with houses for workers on the estate of the Duke of Hamilton; when coal pits were sunk and rows of miners houses were erected the population increased to around 1,300. After the coal seams were exhausted the rows were knocked down and the population shrank to around 500. Reports now appearing in newspapers state that extensive new housing developments are to be allowed in the area. These were hitherto prohibited as it was designated to be part of the green belt. The tram in the photograph belonged to Lanarkshire Tramways, which ran several services including one linking Uddingston and Larkhall via Hamilton. This commenced in 1905, and fares cost from a penny to threepence. Competition from burgeoning private bus services resulted in the gradual abandonment of the system and trams serving Larkhall were withdrawn in September 1928. In the early days of the buses, firms operating out of Larkhall included Frame's (Pioneer), Perrie's (Excel) and Johnson. These small companies were subsequently snapped up by and amalgamated with the Central SMT.

This picture shows the state of the passageway at the rear of the miners' rows at Allanton, just a little further south of Ferniegair and nearer to Larkhall. A group is obtaining water from the common pump and the mucky ground would defy even the most proud housewife's attempts to keep her floors clean. The houses had no running water or electricity and families had shared washhouses and dry closets. Homes had either one room or two. Their tenants were employed in the collieries belonging to the Duke of Hamilton, who received sixpence for every ton of coal dug from the thousands of acres of reserves he owned.

Hamilton Palace

The living conditions of the families at Allanton contrasted sharply with those enjoyed by the Duke of Hamilton and his family at their residence just two miles away. The building of Hamilton Palace commenced in 1592 and succeeding dukes added large extensions until the complex had around 300 rooms. The palace eventually proved too costly to maintain and after permission was given by the Hamilton family to extract coal from under the building, weakening its foundations, it was decided to demolish the entire structure in the early 1920s. The task took eight years to accomplish. This view of the rear of the palace is rarer than pictures showing the front.

Larkhall comprised the lands of Broomhill, Raploch, East Machan and West Machan and the early village grew up around this cross, which is still the hub of the village. The crossroads are formed by the meeting of London Street and Union Street, with Raploch Street running off to the west and Wellgate Street to the east. Externally, the buildings have changed little since this postcard was produced almost 100 years ago; internally all have been modernised. The water pump would have been one of many strategically located along the streets of the village, and such pumps were a great improvement over the old wells which existed beforehand. There is a refreshing absence of cars in the picture that many modern photographers would appreciate when trying to take a street scene or townscape!

UNION ST. LARKHALL.

Nearly a hundred years on it is difficult to comprehend the impact that the tramcars introduced by Lanarkshire Tramways made on the lives of those living in the towns and villages of mid-Lanarkshire. For instance, Larkhall men who prior to the introduction of tram services had to walk to their employment at the collieries at Allanton and Ferniegair could now travel to and from work at a reasonable cost (although some were known to walk in order to save two pence per day, wages being so little). The frequency of the trams compared with the sparse passenger services on the railways meant that housewives could journey to Hamilton for any specialised shopping they required whenever they chose to do so.

Trinity Church, Larkhall seen from the area where King Street was later constructed. This formed the thoroughfare to the Caledonian Railway's Larkhall Central station which opened in 1905. Trinity Church moved to this site from a building in Wellgate Street, now used as a Masonic Hall, in 1901. Designed by Cullen, the famous Hamilton architect, the church cost £7,512.12.1 and is renowned for its fine stained glass windows.

The Revd Walker, minister at Trinity Church, started the Girls Guildry in December 1936. It continues to function today as the Girls Brigade, and has proved to be a very successful venture with many joining as young girls and staying within the movement to become officers. This picture shows members of the Girls Guildry in the 1940s.

Back row: E. McClements, Margaret Scott, Ann Hampson, Rena Wood, Nancy Cameron, Jenny Glassford, Margaret Cochrane, Jean Ferguson, Jan Craw
Third row: Jessie Tudhope (leader), Jean Thomson, Helen Wallace, Maisie Wallace, Nan Cunningham, Margaret McLean, Nettie Hamilton, unknown, unknown, Margaret Gibson, Elizabeth Ramage, Mattie Smith, Betty McLaughlan, Annie McKechnie, May Lawson, Mary Sorbie (teacher)
Second row: Margaret Gillon, Elizabeth Rowe, Nancy Davidson, N. Williamson, Isobel Gillespie, Laura Scott, Margaret Kennedy, Martha Gillon, Miss Telfer (teacher)
Front row: Maisie McIntyre, Margaret Campbell, unknown, Betty Currie, Bessie Hinshelwood, Sadie Moore, Christine Wight

Trinity Church has had a very active unit of the Boys Brigade for over sixty years. This is the company parading to the church in the 1950s led by Captain Tom Davidson and followed by (from the left) Joe Martin, Bobby McGregor and John Currie. Others who can be recognised include David Muir, Billy Strang, John Thomson, Jim Sneddon and Jim Laird.

A photograph of the Boys Brigade dating from 1949. The officers with caps, supervising the boys, are (from the left) George Craig, Tom Banks, Tom Miller and Tom Davidson.

These two Gala Day photographs date from fifty years ago, when community endeavour in Larkhall seemed to be running high. Many local organisations prepared entries for the gala day processions, and crowds lined the streets which were festooned with bunting. The pictures show the town's two bands, Larkhall Town Silver Band and Larkhall Pipe Band, as well as decorated lorries and the Gala Queen and her retinue. She would be crowned either at Morgan Glen or in the Robert Smillie Memorial Park.

Sadly the gala days have now stopped and the two bands are defunct. Another eagerly anticipated event was 'Larkie Fair', held in Bryce's Park at the end of June each year when the noise and bright lights of the 'shows' made for a festive weekend. This, too, has been discontinued and some of the thrills that children enjoyed at gala days and the fair appear to have been lost forever.

Prior to local government reorganisation in 1975, the Fourth District Council of the County of Lanark (based in Larkhall) was very progressive and brought various types of entertainment to the village at both Morgan Glen and Robert Smillie Park. Many will recall interesting days of jousting displays and parachute jumping, along with various sports events. This picture shows a popular train called The Gulliver which ran for several hundred yards from a station appropriately named Lilliput. On the right is the magnificent entrance to Broomhill House. In 1957 a ceremony presided over by John Ewing took place here to dedicate the opening of the Robert Smillie Memorial Park. The speeches of the guests, including local MP Tom Fraser, Emmanuel Shinwell MP and Abe Moffat, president of the Scottish Miners' Union, paid tribute to the work undertaken nationally and internationally by Robert Smillie for workers everywhere. Within the precincts of the park stand Larkhall Academy and Larkhall Leisure Centre, as well as spacious playing fields and football pitches.

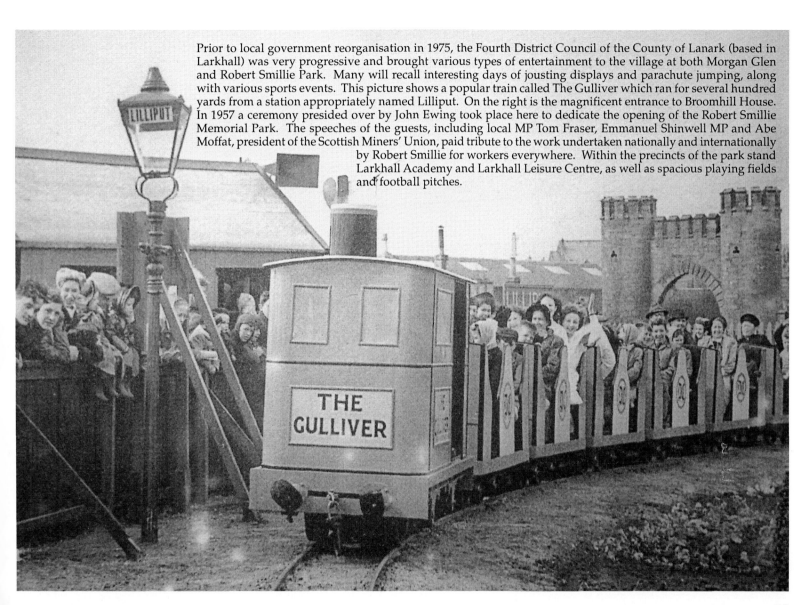

Larkhall East Station

Dalserf station (below), originally called Ayr Road, was used by growers for transporting fruit to the towns as well as for the movement of coal. It was on the same line as Larkhall East. At Dalserf there was a short branch line allowing traffic to reach Stonehouse. Goods trains moved pig iron for smelting to the Jackson Elphick factory at Birkenshaw, as well as collecting the products (baths and other iron castings) the factory made. As this picture shows Cornsilloch Colliery was near Dalserf station. The line was busy with coal trains coming from Coalburn, Auchenheath, Fence and Netherburn pits and Jack McDonald, who worked at the station in the late 1930s, said the trains seemed to run nose to tail towards the marshalling yards at Ross near Hamilton. In contrast Ian Edmiston, relief stationmaster at Dalserf in the 1950s, said he only had to deal with two freight trains per day.

As early as 1800 Larkhall had several short wagonways for horse-drawn wagons at Raploch Collieries and Skellyton Pit, but it was not until 1 December 1856 that the first railway line to run through Dalserf parish came into use. This initially ran from Brocketsbrae to Ferniegair, with a stop at Larkhall, but later continued northwards to Motherwell and Hamilton and southwards to Bankend (Coalburn). The line was mainly used for goods traffic, especially coal, although passenger services were introduced in 1866. The station at Larkhall (which was renamed Larkhall East in 1905) closed to passengers in 1951 and freight in 1964.

Dalserf Railway Station

Netherburn Railway Station.

The 'East Line' (which included the stations at Larkhall East, Dalserf and Netherburn) was built by the Lesmahagow Guarantee Railway Company on behalf of various companies which required a reliable means of transporting coal extracted from the south Lanarkshire coalfield. Some years after opening, the line was taken over by the Caledonian Railway Company, and later under amalgamation in 1923, by the London, Midland & Scottish Railway. A survey of passengers using Netherburn station revealed that in 1950 the average number travelling daily was a mere 14, and it was therefore no surprise that the East Line closed to passenger traffic in 1951. Bungalows now cover the site of Netherburn station.

Larkhall gained another station when a second line was built serving the town. This ran from Ferniegair to Coalburn and included stops at Larkhall, Stonehouse, Blackwood and Lesmahagow. The new station was called Larkhall Central, and this picture shows it on 23 July 1953 with the 6.10 p.m. train (engine number 42166) from Glasgow Central en route to Coalburn. The signalman is standing on the platform waiting to exchange the tablet with the engine driver. Possession of the tablet gave the train, travelling along a single line, the right to proceed to the next station at Stonehouse. The line was officially opened on 1 July 1905, although the section between Larkhall and Stonehouse came into use on 30 June, which was Larkhall Fair Day. Trains ran for most of the day allowing passengers to go to the fair, although for many travelling across the magnificent new viaducts at Larkhall and Stonehouse and enjoying the panoramic views was more important. The new stations at Larkhall Central, Stonehouse, Blackwood and Lesmahagow were built from brick and wood with neat lines and were a great improvement compared to those erected earlier on the East Line. Passenger traffic ceased in 1965 and good services were withdrawn in 1968 when Auchlochan No. 9 Colliery at Coalburn ceased production.

Joseph Hampson was stationmaster at Larkhall Central and Larkhall East in the 1940s. This photograph was taken in 1920 and shows the uniform of a relief stationmaster issued by the Caledonian Railway Company. Mr Hampson is sporting the traditional pocket watch with Albert chain.

When one takes a casual look over the bridge in McNeil Street at the site of Larkhall Central station, now invaded by weeds, scrub and trees, it is difficult to believe that less that forty years ago it was a thrang place in the mornings and evenings. Trains left before 9 a.m. for Glasgow Central station bearing gentlemen travelling to work in offices (many of them employed by British Rail) and young lasses going to typing pools; the 5.10 and 6.11 p.m. trains disgorged the returning commuters back to their homes.

The age of steam driven locomotives pulling passenger trains ended in Scotland in 1967. This picture shows a passenger service crossing Broomhill viaduct at Morgan Glen, Larkhall in the 1950s. Arrol Bros. of Glasgow built the viaduct, which in its day was considered to be a monumental piece of engineering. Still standing but no longer in use, it was the highest railway bridge in Scotland, standing 170 feet above the River Avon with a total length of 530 feet. It was erected on bases of concrete 52 feet long by 32 feet and sunk between 25 and 60 feet underground. Not three miles distant was Stonehouse viaduct, which also spanned the River Avon and was demolished several years ago. The Larkhall viaduct should probably be preserved as an outstanding engineering achievement of the railway age, although many parents in the Strutherhill and Birkenshaw estates fear it could be a dangerous attraction to fearless children.

Larkhall Victualling Society was formed in 1821, making it one of the earliest co-operatives to be established in Britain. Its first premises were a house in Hamilton Street, although before 1830 the society had moved to the old grocery shop seen here, which stood adjacent to the branch grocery store in Wellgate Street. Histories of these societies (and there is an excellent history of Larkhall Victualling Society) preached the values of co-operation. However, like other societies in Scotland, Larkhall's did not extend these values to women, who were refused membership until 1894. It is a significant fact that in the first 100 years of the society's existence, no woman was elected to serve on the board of management. In its later years, Larkhall Victualling Society set up youth clubs and in 1951, having won the area and Scottish final in public speaking, their youth club represented Scotland in the British final in London, coming second.

The society built this fine range of shops in Union Street in order to provide more extensive services for its members from a central location. Like many other co-operatives, Larkhall Victualling Society experienced increased competition from supermarkets after the end of the 1939–1945 war, as well as a general change in attitudes to methods of shopping. When it ceased to be viable as an independent organisation it was taken over by the Scottish Co-operative Society. It was sad to see the loss of such a long-established organisation, along with the demolition of its elegant shops and buildings, which have been replaced by a utilitarian structure that does not enhance Larkhall's principal thoroughfare.

The interior of the victualling society's central grocery in Union Street around 1920. Young lads and lasses underwent a five-year apprenticeship to become a grocer. This was not an enviable job as shops were open until 9 p.m. on weekdays and later on Saturdays. Butter, sugar and other basic foods were delivered in bulk to the goods yard at the railway goods station and then brought to the grocery. Staff measured out items like sugar into 1 lb and 2 lb bags. The customer waited while butter was cut, weighed and a design put on top with a butter pat. Cheese was cut with wire slicers. Junior apprentices had unpleasant and smelly jobs allocated to them such as measuring out carbide for miners' lamps and filling oil containers for lamps in pre-electricity days. All the tasks were time-consuming but this was of little consequence as the wages of grocers were so small.

The society had a large bakery housed in this building at the corner of Drygate Street and Wellgate Street (now the premises of a DIY firm), and it seems unbelievable that it should have required as many delivery vans as are shown in this 1920s photograph. The records of the society reveal that it wasn't until 1894 that the decision was reached to introduce the first horse and cart for making deliveries to customers. A horse costing £38 was bought from John Burns of the Commercial Inn. Mr Porter, the local saddler, supplied the necessary harness. Thomas Smith, a coachbuilder, made a light van costing £20.17.6. There were 70 applicants for the post of vanman, revealing the shortage of work locally, 1894 being a year when there was a miners' strike lasting seven months.

Larkhall, which had a lending library as early as 1796, is renowned in Scotland for having formed building societies for the provision of houses for their members at a very early date. The first indication of the weavers showing a spirit of co-operation was the establishment of the Larkhall and Millheugh Friendly Society in 1809. Its members paid a weekly subscription in return for financial benefits when off sick and a sum of money on death. The first building society in Larkhall was set up around 1816 by a small number of men, mainly weavers. Each of the houses, which were built at Pleasance, was a but and a ben with unplastered internal walls, a thatched roof and flagstones for floors. The saying that the proud possessors of the new homes were the 'Bonnet Lairds o' Larkie' originated because of the weavers' involvement in building them. This picture shows the first house in High Pleasance to be built by Larkhall Building Society.

These houses in Miller Street were built following the establishment of Larkhall's second building society around 180 years ago. Externally they remain the same, but the interiors have been modernised and extensions built to the rear. The cross marks the house that belonged to Robert Smillie, Larkhall's most famous son. In the succeeding years Larkhall formed several more building societies, the most modern of which were the Cherryhill View Building Societies that operated from 1892 to 1937.

On the left of this picture is Meadowhill or 'The Buffy'. Just beyond is the site of Larkhall library which is roughly where Beattie's School stood before being knocked down. The stone-built houses on the right, now the site of an open space, went by the name of 'Dookity Dyke', possibly because the upper story looked like pigeon lofts.

Both this photograph and the one above show rows of miners houses that have been demolished. Merryton Rows at Lanark Road End were built for workers at Merryton Colliery.

Back row: Agnes Miller, Dr Burns (for 21 years service as medical practitioner to the firm), John Ballantyne, Tom Little, David Marley, M. Goodman (42 years service – second watch), David Grant, George Smith, Bertie Whip

Front row: Margaret Calderwood, Molly Gibney, Marion Law, Betty Hodge, Dr Simpson (proprietor of firm), Ann Miller, A. Weir, Mattie Davidson

Daks Simpson, manufacturers of high quality jackets, trousers, suits and overcoats, have been the major local employer for over fifty years. The firm came to Larkhall in 1940 after their premises in London suffered bomb damage. They moved into the unused accommodation of the old silk factory in Miller Street, and having been given a regional grant to help ease the problem of unemployment in Larkhall, built premises on their present site in 1948. In 1969 the factory was extended to 183,000 square feet. Their products proved popular and at one time the firm employed nearly 2,000 people. In recent years the loss of a long-term contract to supply Marks and Spencer, combined with increasing competition from cheaper foreign imports, has led to hundreds of staff being paid off. It is the custom for Daks Simpson to present employees with watches for 21 years service, and this photograph shows a group of staff after receiving their awards in April 1974.

Back row: R. Dick,
G. Hamilton,
G. Millar,
J. Ramage,
T. Perrie
Front row: J. Laird,
T. Simpson,
W. Baillie,
R. Frame

Larkhall had a Miners' Welfare Institute from the 1920s and this provided a centre for indoor recreation and a large hall for dances and concerts. Adjoining the premises was a sports pavilion with changing facilities for the players on two tennis courts and two bowling greens. Larkhall Miners' Welfare Tennis Club was very successful and the photograph shows the players who won the Lanarkshire League Championship in 1959. As was the case with so many tennis clubs, interest in the sport waned and it was disbanded, the courts being converted into a car park for the bowling greens as more and more bowlers travelled by car to play on the greens. (Photograph by kind permission of Studio Paris, Larkhall.)

L to R: Agnes Baillie, Betty Smith, Meg Frame, Greta Swarbrick, Peggy McFadyen, Kate Cowan, Cathie Meek, Bunty Dickson, Nan Cross, Jessie Goray

Larkhall has two bowling clubs with greens less than a hundred yards from each other. Larkhall Miners' Welfare Bowling Club continued under that name from the 1920s until around 1980 when the halls of the miners' welfare institute were demolished. Thereafter the name was changed to Raploch Bowling Club to differentiate it from Larkhall Bowling Club whose premises are at Crossgates. The photograph shows cup winners of Larkhall Miners' Welfare Bowling Club in 1976.

Larkhall was among the first places in Lanarkshire outwith the large towns to have a leisure centre. This opened in 1964 and initially had a swimming pool and sports barn with five badminton courts. The facilities allowed twenty players to be on court at any one time and reflected progress from the days of playing in church halls with four on court and many waiting their chance to participate. This picture shows some members of the Avondale Badminton Club in 1986.

Back row: Bill Broadbent, Cheryl Letham, David Coffee, David Letham, John Stewart, Alan Smith, Frank Turnbull, John Keeper, Jim Pollock, Eric Murray, Jack Smith, George Alston, Joe Mackay, Ian Dickson, Sandra Dickson
Front row: Pat Barnes, Jim Brown, Maureen Hamilton, Val Stewart, Rae Cunningham, Marjorie Mackay

Back row: Mrs Pringle, Betty Lowson, Mrs D. Muirhead (and Craig), Graeme Muirhead, Danny Wardlaw, Jack Smith, David Ewing, Stewart McDonald, Gordon Miller, Andrew Law, Margaret Devine, Stewart Clarkson, Donald Muirhead, May Eadie, Ann Simpson, Fiona Archibald, Stewart Lowson
Front row: Martin Muirhead, Neil Paris, Malcolm Paris (and dog Tara), Stephen Scott, Adrian Wood, Elaine Miller, unknown, Penny Graham, Elizabeth Smith, Ann Perrie, Graham Hamilton, Millar Hamilton, Simon Muirhead

Soon after his appointment as baths master, Donald Muirhead built up a reputation for training fine swimmers and running a popular swimming club. The photograph shows participants on a ten mile sponsored walk held to raise money for club funds on 8 March 1970. (Photograph by kind permission of Studio Paris, Larkhall.)

Back: Weldon, Houston, McInnes, Lennie, Young, Hamilton
Front: Rae, Hutton, Galloway, Brown, Harvie

Football has always had widespread support in Larkhall and the village has produced very many players, too numerous to list individually, who have left the junior ranks, gone senior and gained international caps. However mention must be made of three dynasties that have brought fame to the village – the families of Gibson, McStay and McLean. As well as having juvenile teams and a ladies' team, Larkhall once had four junior teams, two of which still survive. The oldest is Larkhall Thistle, which since its formation in 1878 has played at Gasworks Park. Royal Albert was formed by an amalgamation of two teams, Larkhall and Plotcock, and took its unusual name from a yacht belonging to Captain Boyd of Mafflat who had been generous with support for the new club. Royal Albert originally played at Raploch Park which had a dog track round it, moving in 1960 when the land was sold for housing to play in the council-owned Robert Smillie Memorial Park. Royal Albert was actually a senior team until season 1928/9 when they reverted back to playing in the junior league. Both Royal Albert and Larkhall Thistle continue to attract strong support and loyal affection, which helps the teams through good and bad times. This picture shows a successful Royal Albert team in season 1960/61.

Back row: A. Simpson, W. Falconer, B. Falconer, H. Penman, J. McManus, Mrs Findlay (hall keeper at Birkenshaw Miners Welfare Institute)
Front row: J. Nelson, W. Moore, W. Penman, D. Douglas, B. Findlay

Quoiting was once a popular sport throughout Scotland and Larkhall has the current Scottish champion – Billy Falconer – who represents the Birkenshaw Club, the only surviving club playing the sport in Lanarkshire. In fact there are now only seven clubs in Scotland – Dunnottar at Stonehaven (the players are farmers), Linwood, Kirkconnel, Canonbie, Gretna and Glenburn (Prestwick). Birkenshaw Club, which originated in the 1920s, became defunct in the 1960s but was started again in 1979 and now has at least 40 members supporting it and 20 playing regularly. Birkenshaw has been top in the Scottish team championship 23 times since 1930, while Larkhall Raploch, whose ground was in Raploch Street opposite the Victory Bar on a site now used for housing, was Scottish champion three times before folding. Four players form a team for the Scottish championship, the winners being the team whose members score most points. Most clubs have four rinks, all with two heads. The standard distance for throwing is now 18 yards and as the quoits are heavy (weighing around 5 lb) players need skill, dexterity and strength. Fifty or more years ago, nearly every mining village had at least one club and games could attract many spectators who often bet on the outcome of the match, as well as having side bets on who would win an end. Big tournaments were held at different locations on each day of the Glasgow Fair Fortnight; Birkenshaw Club hired a double deck bus to take players, supporters and families to venues such as at Annan for a pleasant day out. Such was the enthusiasm for quoiting in the Depression years of the 1920s and 1930s that at the rear of several of the buildings at Birkenshaw, small areas for two rinks would be set aside where players could practice, and there was strong inter-building rivalry. All that was needed was an iron pin and a square yard of clay. Information about the Birkenshaw Club was given to me by Boyd Falconer who has won the Scottish singles championship six times (his brother Billy has won it nine times). On more than one occasion they have contested the Scottish singles final. Both assured me that their uncle, Willie Penman, was 'the daddy of them all' having won the Scottish title fifteen times before he emigrated to Canada where he died several years ago. This picture shows the Scottish cup winners for seasons 1961 and 1962.

Class 2B at Larkhall Academy in Academy Street during session 1942–3. Ambrose Burns, a member of the class who was unfortunately off sick when the photograph was taken, loaned this print to me. Ambrose also showed me a photograph of the joint class of boys and girls for session 1945–6, (the fourth year class) with only 12 boys and 6 girls having decided to continue their education, the others having left at the permitted age of 14 years. Many would have been forced to sacrifice their education in order to work to help the family finances. The names of the class members were Archibald Hamilton, James Brown, James Forrest, Charles Hodge, Ambrose Burns, James Perrie, William Sinclair, George Brownlie, Ronald Nicholson, Gourlay Black, James Harris, Elizabeth Bradford, Euphemia Kennedy, Mary Reid, Agnes Henderson, Mary Bell, Helen Morton and John Moodie.

Larkhall Academy, First Year Class 1945.

Back row: Mary Laird, Helen Kirkwood, Isobel Lindsay, Ella Davidson, Helen Lawson, Georgina Gibson, Helen Melvin, Isobel Muir
Third row: Isobel Cunningham, May McNicol, Elma Little, Jenny Coutts, Ellison McInnes, Betty Woods, Mary Monie, Jean Barclay, Helen Mason
Second row: Isobel McCulloch, Jean Harker, Joyce Scott, Helen McEwan, Agnes Anderson, Janet Hair, Margaret Frame, Betty Brown, Rena Cunningham
Front row: Ella Kellighan, Marion Semple, Bethia Miller, Margaret Anderson

New Academy, Larkhall.

Larkhall Academy at its former location in Academy Street. Many who attended this school regret the decision to demolish such a substantial sandstone building and feel that efforts should have been made to use it for a worthwhile purpose. Larkhall Academy was first established in Union Street in 1874 for primary and secondary pupils, following the passing of the Education (Scotland) Act in 1872. The school had a staff of four teachers, assisted by five monitors, to look after 500 pupils. Subjects taught were writing, arithmetic, bookkeeping and drawing; by 1875 these had been augmented by Latin, French, sewing and mapping (on Saturday mornings). Since its establishment the rectors have included Messrs Brown, Thomson, Haddow, Cameron, Lochhead, Herbison, Thomson and Dingwall. The present school is fed by nine primary schools: Machanhill, Craigbank, Robert Smillie, Glengowan, Hareleeshill, Newfield (Stonehouse), Stonehouse, Dalserf and Netherburn. In earlier years there were schools at Duke Street, Muir Street, Shawburn and Toll (Canderside). At present Larkhall Academy has a roll of 1,150 with 86 full- or part-time teaching staff, plus two librarians, eight members of an office and administrative team and four technicians.

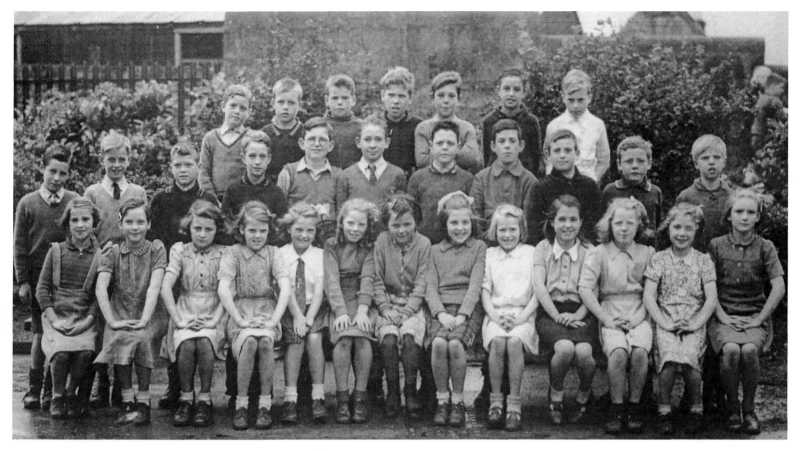

Back row: Alex McLuskie, Francy Markie, Pat O'Donnell, Hugh Clarke, Robert Burns, Frank Gibney, Tommy Wedlock
Middle row: Thomas Brannigan, Benny Lafferty, Andy Riley, David McMunn, John Berry, Jim O'Neill, Hugh Crainey, Phil Bryson, John McGourt, Tommy Farr, James Thompson
Front row: Margaret McGowan, Anna Campbell, Cathie Connor, Isa Egan, Chrissie McQueen, Cathie McLaren, May Gordon, Eileen Smith, May McKay, Mary Goldie, May McLaughlin, Mary McDonald, May Laughlin

Class 4 at St Mary's Primary School, Larkhall, in 1944–5. From 1846, when a Roman Catholic mission was established for Hamilton and the surrounding area, Mass was celebrated in Scanlon's Hotel in Raploch Street, Larkhall. In 1872 a Chapel School was opened and in 1905 a new church was built at Braehead. Now there is a congregation of over 1,000 parishioners attached to St Mary's Chapel.

Chalmers Church Choir, 1958–59.

Back row: J. Moodie, J. Smith, I. Robertson, J. Reid, A. Smith,
J. Lee, D. Scott, J. McClue
Third row: D. Perrie, R. Miller, H. Simpson, M. Evans,
I. Edmiston, M. Bell, I. Leckie, B. Carnihan, A. Miller,
M. Rundell, J. McDonald, M. Stirrat, A. Bell, J. Scott
Second row: M. Laird, E. Edmiston, T. Miller, P. Strang,
M. Grieve, J. Leckie, M. Simpson, M. Grieve, M. Strang,
A. Peat
Front row: M. Moore, A. Miller, K. McFarlane,
J. Roe, Hugh Rundell (choirmaster), Revd J. McNay,
L. Milne, I. Simpson, A. Colquhoun, M. Evans

Right: This picture shows the original Chalmers Church in Union Street (the modern church is at Strutherhill). At the time of the centenary celebrations in 1960 it saddened church members that they had to decide to give up worshipping in the church they loved. However, as there were three places of worship for the Church of Scotland within a hundred yards on Larkhall's main street it seemed Christian-like to relocate and provide a church for the huge estates of Strutherhill and Birkenshaw. The utilitarian building opened in 1961 at Strutherhill contrasts sharply with the original Chalmers Church. Like Larkhall Academy, the old church is another building that might have been adapted for other purposes rather than suffer demolition, and its removal has deprived central Larkhall of an architectural asset that enhanced Union Street for a century.

Back row: Alex Colquhoun, George Rundell, Ken Neilson, Jack Dunsmore (twin), Linda Hamilton, Ena Lang, Marion Dunsmore (twin), James Hunter, Jim Somerville, William Sneddon, Tom Durham, Alan Gibson, Mrs Kirkwood
Third row: Billy Mackay, Agnes Deans, Margaret Bell, Rona Fortune, Elizabeth Edgar (twin), Margaret Edgar (twin), Margaret Frame, Grace Faulds, Emma Bryson (twin), Shona McLuskie, Eileen Dickson, Sandy Marshall
Second row: Robert McCutcheon (twin), Jimmy Dunsmore, Catherine Bell, Marion Cowan, May Gilfillan, Ann McDonald, Betty Bell, Caroline Stewart, Jean Falconer, Ann Hill, Sandra Dickson, Danny Hampson, Archie Fulton
Front row: Jim Cossar, Archie Burton, Ronald Ferguson, Ross Fulton, John Logan, Charles McCutcheon (twin), Jim Torrance, Robert Rowan
(Absent through sickness, Robert Bryson (twin))

Craigbank Primary School was one of two schools (the other being Robert Smillie Primary) opened to cope with the large number of children whose families moved into the Strutherhill and Birkenshaw areas following the boom in council house building after the end of the Second World War in 1945. This picture shows the primary one class at Craigbank in March 1961.

Craigbank Primary School.

A favourite Sunday walk for many generations was to leave Larkhall by Raploch Street or McNeil Street and descend the steep hill to Millheugh, possibly returning to the village either by the Morgan Glen or Mary Hoses. (In the absence of any more likely tale, this path allegedly takes its name from Mary, Queen of Scots losing a stocking in the vicinity while staying at the old castle at Chatelherault.)

Millheugh. Larkhall

Millheugh was the picnic area for Larkhall parents and children on summer days, where they could play at the ford on the River Avon and enjoy their sandwiches and 'ginger'. Its fame was not merely confined to Larkhall and Sunday school outings would make the banks very busy on Saturdays, as old postcards prove.

This view of Millheugh shows the lade (running below the wall to the left of the river), which took water from the Avon to the nearby bleachfield. One of the buildings above it is the Applebank Inn (opened as an alehouse in 1714) which provided food and drink for travellers using the horse-drawn coaches between Hamilton, Larkhall and Stonehouse. On the horizon is Broomhill House, home to a long line of families which were offshoots of the ducal Hamiltons, including the McNeil-Hamiltons. The histories of many villages include a mysterious 'dark', 'black' or 'green' lady and the villagers of Larkhall seem to have some basis for believing that a lady of Asian descent lived at Broomhill House for some years from 1902 before unexpectedly disappearing. Some believe that her ghost haunts the Broomhill ruins, although a television crew with cameras failed to record any evidence to back up the story. Once a favourite area for walkers, Morgan Glen suffered from rubbish dumping for many years, although efforts are currently being made to return it to its former attractive state. It was originally gifted to Larkhall by Captain Morgan of the Applebank Inn. The old brig, built in 1790 to replace the ford, was washed away in a storm in 1934. Towering high in the background is Broomhill viaduct.

The explanation of why Larkhall is humorously referred to as 'Dawsonville' or 'Dawson City' goes back nearly a century. At the foot of Muir Street (seen below in the leisurely age of the horse and carriage), where it joins Drygate Street was Meadowhill, an area of several miners' rows referred to by former residents as 'The Buffy'. A poem by an unknown author called *The Buffy Ballad* lists many of the residents, indicating that some were eccentric characters, the best remembered of which is Harry Dawson. A couplet in the poem states:

We'd Harry Dawson roon the front, who ran cairts cheek fur cheek
He's deid, puir soul; nae mair we'll see his great big girr and cleek.

MUIR ST. LARKHALL.

Harry (left) is remembered in Larkhall to this day and two stories persist some 76 years after his death. He roamed the streets with his huge girr propelled by a cleek and once ran to Glasgow with them. It is alleged he said on his return home that he lost his girr in Glasgow so he had to walk back to Larkhall. The other story concerns his retort to his mother one winter morning. She had intended to wake Harry's brother who slept in the same bed as him, but inadvertently disturbed Harry who told her 'I don't work, mither, I'm daft', and then went back to sleep. His brother had to rise and put on his working clothes, catch a train at 6 a.m. to Coalburn and do an eight hour shift underground. In January 1925, when aged 35 years, Harry died in Glasgow Royal Infirmary from injuries suffered when he stepped in front of a bus in London Street, Larkhall. His memory lingers on, just like the often quoted saying that the long wall which stretches from near Hamilton to Larkhall was constructed to 'keep the daft folk in Larkhall' – only to be answered by 'it was to keep the daft folk out'.

Back row: W. Yule, J. McLean, J. Fullarton, J. McFarlane, Don Fullarton, J. Simmonds, W. Sloan
Middle row: H. Walker (secretary), J. Jackson, P. Grenfell, W. Greenhorn, F. McAlevy, P. Jones, G. Elliot, W. McCutcheon
Front row: J. Tait, G. Smith, A. Fullarton, C. Telfer, J. McLeod, D. Fullarton, Harry Scott

Although Larkhall was never designated a town, Larkhall Town Band existed from early in the last century until the 1930s. The band broke up because of a variety of factors; these included lack of finance, as it did not have a colliery or manufacturer behind it, and the 'poaching' of the best players by bands offering inducements such as well-paid jobs and housing. After the 1939–45 war a nucleus of former players such as the Fullarton family got together and the band was reformed. It had a very active women's committee under the late Jean Gillespie which raised a lot of money for instruments and music. The band had more than twenty years of success, during which time it won the Scottish Amateur Band Association Championship finals and took part in the British championship at the Albert Hall in London. When permission to rent the hall used for some decades by the band at Gallowhill was withdrawn it proved disastrous, as a regular practice base is so essential. By the 1970s the band was failing to attract players and reluctantly the committee agreed to disband it. The instruments were eventually handed over to Larkhall Academy for its music classes. Over the years the band was served by many excellent professional conductors such as John Faulds, George Hawkins and Charles Telfer, and by bandmasters including Archibald Harris and William Brown. Hugh Walker, the secretary and mainstay of the band for many years, was awarded a life membership award for fifty years' service to the Scottish Amateur Band Association. Although the village has had flute bands over the years the Larkhall Pipe and Drum Band is no longer in existence either. This picture shows Larkhall Town Band in the 1950s.

Left: The butcher's shop at Charing Cross belonged to the maternal great-grandfather of Gavin Wilson, current proprietor of Burns the Stationers. From left to right the people in the picture are Christine Clark (who became Mrs Robertson), William (Wull) Paterson, who has a son still living in Larkhall, and Mrs G. Watson, Gavin Wilson's maternal grandmother.

Tarmacadam being laid on Machan Brae in the early 1900s when this was the main highway between Glasgow and Carlisle. Photographs of the collieries in Larkhall are very scarce and this print is valuable in showing the location of Broomhill No. 3 Colliery with its chimney and winding gear. Several pits in Larkhall and Netherburn were known by the nickname of 'Juck', a name used by the miners because they had to work in wet conditions only suitable for ducks.

Three rows containing 36 houses surrounded Summerlee Pit, according to my informant Maggie Deans (M. S. Hay) who lived there as a girl and for a period after her marriage. 'By the time I was born, we had a house with two very small bedrooms, a kitchen, a scullery and an inside WC. Before that the houses had shared dry toilets situated some distance from the entrance door. All three rooms had a built-in bed. Mither had a hard time when it came to washing clothes. There were six washhouses for the 36 houses so you began your allocated day early by kindling the boiler fire. The washing was done in a bine (wooden tub) and we used White Windsor soap we bought in the co-operative store. Ye needed a lot o' elbow grease. And washing was often easier than getting the clothes dried. We had

a drying green we could use in the days that werena' raining but more often than not, the weekly washing had to be dried on the pulley or on winter dykes at the fire.' Maggie Deans told me about her first job. 'I worked on the screes at Summerlee picking the dirt out of the coal. Our hours were 7 a.m. until 3.30 p.m. For that filthy work I got eighteen shillings each week and that was for toiling six days every week. Nae paid holidays. There were always about a half dozen girls like me aged fourteen years and upwards working alongside the boys at the dirt picking. We wore a patchy apron, dust cap and heavy boots. There were nae pitheid baths. We went home ingrained with coal dust and in our house I had to wash in the scullery or the wash house as my father and brothers got cleaned up in a tin bath in front of the living-room fire.' After two years Maggie transferred to working on a farm where the hours were 7 a.m. until 5 p.m. Some of the work was healthy and enjoyable like collecting the harvest but she will never forget the toil during the winter months such as trying to dig out or kick out turnips frozen into the ground so that they could be shawed and tailed.

Back row: Nancy Tannock, Jean Scott, Jenny Tannock, Isa Faulds
Front row: Robina McMillan, Mary Potter, Agnes Meikle, Mary Scott, Maggie Hay, Maggie McMillan, Marion Potter, Marion Hynds

This group of girls was photographed at Summerlee Rows in the 1920s. Note the style of dress, short haircuts and 'Nora Battey' style stockings.

Left: Agnes Hay and Annie Rae photographed in front of a railway wagon before starting surface work at Summerlee Colliery in the 1920s.

The tenants of the houses at Summerlee Rows in 1948 just a few years prior to their demolition were as follows (the numbers refer to the house numbers): 1 John Clark, 2 John Fallow, 3 John Ramage, 4 Annie Cowan, 5 Thomas Ramage, 6 George Carbray, 7 Agnes Mair, 8 Andrew Scott, 9 John Hay, 10 Thomas Carbray, 11 Gavin Craw, 12 George Bolton, 13 William Potter, 14 Robert Morton, 15 Michael Burns, 16 Thomas Jackson, 17 Thomas Logan, 18 Sarah Carbray, 19 William McMillan, 20 James Horne, 21 John Potter, 22 Samuel Barclay, 23 William Barclay, 24 hall belonging to Hebron Christian Brethren, 25 John Sneddon, 26 John Gillon, 27 Charles McDonald, 28 David Brown, 29 Jean Cunningham, 30 Robert Potter, 31 Andrew Scott, 32 Margaret Hay, 33 George Deans, 34 Annie Rae, 35 Robert Wiseman.

A rural scene at Burnhead on the outskirts of Larkhall on the road to Ashgill and Netherburn. On the right just at the brig was a small coal mine belonging to Mr Burns that was still operational around 1950. On the left at the rear of the double row of stone-built houses known as Colvin's Buildings is Larkhall Golf Course, run by South Lanarkshire Council. Prior to the outbreak of war in 1939 this was a nine hole private golf course, but was closed during the war when the site was used for the opencast extraction of coal.

Rorison Memorial Church at Ashgill. The church has an active congregation, with meetings of the Boys Brigade, Girls Brigade, Youth Fellowship and Women's Guild. Ashgill began to grow from the 1850s onwards (a post office opened in 1899), increasing in size as collieries were developed. The three main collieries were Cornsilloch, Dalserf and Woodside (the latter was between Ashgill and Netherburn), all of which erected rows of houses for their employees. These rows were knocked down in the 1920s and 1930s when the centre of the village was consolidated with the erection of council houses. Since the 1960s Ashgill has increased in size with the building of many villas and bungalows. The village had four sets of tomato houses, which closed when the cost of heating these proved uneconomical against competition from cheaper foreign imports. Many local residents – including children during their summer holidays – found employment in the market gardens of the Clyde Valley, especially during the strawberry and plum seasons. Ashgill and Shawsburn had 1,151 voters in the year 2000.

The hamlet of Swinhill lies between Garrion Bridge and Canderside Toll on the A71. This picture was taken in the early 1920s before the demolition of the miners' rows on the left in 1928. William Roy's shop sold second-hand goods, and was well used in the Depression years of the 1920s. The building next to the shop with the woman at the door had the unusual title for a building in a mining community of Swinhill and Birkenshaw Liberal Club Hall. George Feeney, who lived in Swinhill, remembers how his parents brought up ten children in a room and kitchen house with a scullery. Water was obtained by the tenants from three water pumps so had to be carried in, with waste water carried out again to the sheugh running parallel to the road. Gas was provided, but there wasn't an electricity supply. There were dry closets at the rear and the contents were regularly emptied by the farmer onto his fields. George's father, who died at 50 from a miner's disease (leaving his widow to rear the family, six of whom were still at or under school age), washed every day after his stint at the pit with cold water in one of the washhouses. In 1928 the Feeney family moved to the terraced rows, which provided a higher standard of comfort and stood until 1968. When the colliery stopped production in 1942 and the manager's house with three bedrooms became empty it was allocated to Mrs Feeney. She accepted the tenancy because of its improved spaciousness and the flitting (removal) was undertaken using a cart without a horse – her sons pulled the vehicle. She only stayed in her new home one night, insisting on returning to live in the terraces to be beside her former neighbours. The horseless cart was used again. In 1968 Swinhill terraces were demolished and their occupants rehoused in Larkhall. Only a few cottages and the Swinhill Miners' Welfare Institute (erected in 1924) still stand today. Rab Dunbar looks after the institute, an unpaid labour of love, mainly to provide a place of recreation for young lads who like to play snooker and can only afford a nominal charge. The days of Swinhill being a mining community with an annual gala day are just a memory to former residents. George Feeney wrote a nostalgic poem about life and the inhabitants of Swinhill. Here are four lines:

Where are the Swinhill weans who played in the street
At bools, or spin the perrie, or wi' a girr and a cleek,
Hunch cuddy hunch or jumpin' the burn
Played kick the can and then had to run?

This photograph shows of one of the terraces at Swinhill which was demolished in 1968. These consisted of three double rows known simply as the Front Rows, the Middle Rows and the Back Rows. Here are the names of the householders in Swinhill Terraces in 1948, obtained from HM Records Office, Edinburgh: 1 Alexander Hamilton, 2 David Hunter, 3 Gilbert Sim (Jnr.), 4 William Hickie, 5 John Hamilton, 6 Robert Dunbar, 7 Archibald Meek, 8 Nisbet Sim, 9 Thomas Mitchell, 10 George McLean (Jnr.), 11 George McLean, 12 Callum McGhie, 13 Georgina and Edward Feeney, 14 Robert Eaton, 15 Matthew and John Miller, 16 Gilbert B. Sim, 17 David Frame, 18 Robert McKinlay, 19 Margaret and William Murray, 20 Grace Frame, 21 Robert Lang, 22 James McLehose, 23 Thomas Robertson, 24 Alex Brown, 25 James Andrews, 26 Alexander Colquhoun, 27 William Harvey, 28 Samuel Eaton, 29 William Fleming, 30 Andrew Sim, 31 James Sim, 32 James McKinlay, 33 Francis Brown, 34 James Hickie, 35 James Kent, 36 Charles Skinner, 37 Matthew McLuskie, 38 Peter Skinner (Jnr.), 39 Peter McDonald, 40 William Mitchell, 41 Christine Black, 42 John Frame, 43 James Meek, 44 Jane and John Shield, 45 Peter Hunter, 46 Alexander Todd, 47 William Kent, 48 Thomas Clark, 49 Agnes Richmond, 50 William Eaton, 51 John Ferguson, 52 empty.

The mound in the background was Swinhill Colliery bing, where waste dug up with the coal was dumped. The surface workers are:

Back row: Jolly Miller, Jim Campbell, Peter King, William Barclay, Alex McLuckie
Front row: Rab Dunbar, Andrew McKay, unknown.

This is the pug (railway engine) which moved coal wagons to and from Broomfield Colliery near Netherburn. Davie Speedie was the driver and Tommy Adams the brakeman for many years. There were several pugs in use in Larkhall in the first decades of last century and railway lines criss-crossed the village and the surrounding area.

Back row: Billy Sneddon, Frank Struthers, George Falconer, Jim Falconer, John Hogg, John Boles, Willie McPhee, Daniel McLeish

Middle row: Jessie Barclay, Betty Brownhill, Helen Paterson, Helen Semple, Agnes Armstrong, Jane Surgeoner, Margaret Peters, Cathie Thomson

Front row: Jean Gray, Margaret Adams, Helen McAuley, Georgina Russell, Helen Paterson, Isa Falconer, Margaret Falconer, Agnes Currie

On knees: Jim Forrest, Willie McAuley

A class at Netherburn Primary School in 1935. The moorland village of Netherburn lies three miles south of Larkhall in the parish of Dalserf, and owes its existence to rich coal seams found on the Duke of Hamilton's Netherburn Farm. These were worked from the 1830s for around a hundred years. The duke constructed a new road to connect the colliery with the Lanark Road. There were three main pits, Annabella, Woodside and Broomfield, and rows of houses for the incoming miners were huddled around the railway station, which opened in 1856. The village has had a post office since 1880, and from the 1920s Netherburn had a miners' welfare institute providing facilities for concerts, dances and cinema screenings, as well as a room with two full-size billiard tables. It also had a changing room for players using the adjoining football field plus a tennis court, the first in central Lanarkshire with an all-weather surface. The institute lasted some years after the end of the 1939–1945 war before being demolished, but several years passed before a new community hall was built. Nearly fifty years ago a large housing scheme was built for villagers from the condemned rows, as well as an influx of key workers who came to Larkhall to work at factories such as Rolls Royce on the new industrial estates. Over the years Netherburn has had a gala day, an active community council, a horticultural show and a Brownie pack. There have been several colourful characters such as Jimmy Surgeoner, who owned the local pub, made coffins at the rear and pulled teeth at the bar. Like nearly every mining village, Netherburn had a junior then a juvenile football team. One of my informants, septuagenarian Davie Cross, played professional football with Hibernians, Airdrie and Dundee United and he talked about the McStay dynasty who produced generations of top-class players including Jimmy and Paul of Celtic and Scotland. Netherburn is now a rather isolated community with only a few shops and a modern village hall. The Gospel Hall, where services and a Sunday school were provided by volunteers for over 150 years, was demolished in 2000 after the building caught fire.

The Glasgow stance for the Larkhall bus services in the 1920s was in Cathedral Street. Seen here in 1928 when new is VA 8067, a Leyland 'Lion' in the large fleet operated by the Lanarkshire Traction Company Ltd., a sister company of Central SMT which was based in Motherwell.

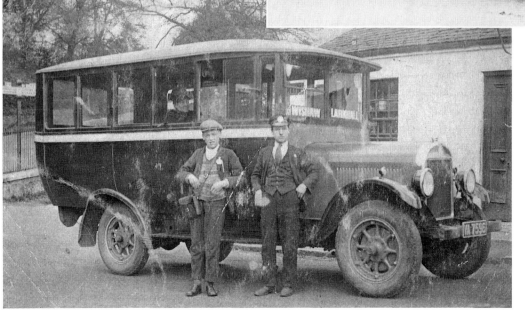

This was the bus which operated between Larkhall and Wishaw in the late 1920s. It was owned by Isaac Hutchison of Overtown, and the company still runs a network of local bus services today in the Larkhall/Wishaw/Motherwell area. VA 7596 was a 14-seater Reo imported from the USA. The photograph was taken en route at the old tollhouse, Garrion Bridge.

James Perrie of Larkhall operated the 'Excel' bus service between Larkhall and Glasgow, and also further out to Lesmahagow and Coalburn. The Perrie brothers had originally been employed as bus drivers by their uncle, William Frame of Larkhall, who had pioneered the Glasgow service (see ticket) but after a dispute, started on their own behalf. This Albion 'Viking' charabanc was pride of the Excel fleet when new in 1926 and was normally used exclusively on touring work, although was occasionally pressed into service to Glasgow. In 1928 the Perrie brothers sold the business to the GOC (Glasgow Omnibus Company), then one of the major bus operators in Lanarkshire.

This picture, dating from about 1925, shows Frame's shop and petrol station in Hamilton Road, Larkhall. It sold Power Petrol and Texaco oils, and the pumps bore the lettering ROP, which prompted children to chant 'rotten old petrol'. The shop also sold sweets, tobacco and general provisions.